**Copyri**

All rights reserved. reproduced, distributed, or transmitted in any form or by any means, including photocopying, recording, or other electronic or mechanical methods, without the prior written permission of the author or publisher, except in the case of brief quotations embodied in critical reviews and certain other noncommercial uses permitted by copyright law. For permission requests regarding this story, contact the author or publisher.

**Printed in the United States of America.**

**First Printing, 2023**

**ISBN: 979-8-9872100-7-9**

## Author

IG: @Uncimo

uncimobooks@gmail.com

## Publisher

IG | FB | Twitter: @wcwriting1

Visit Our Website

Williamscommerce1.com

Williams Commerce, LLC

## **Dedication**

This story is deeper than myself. I would like to dedicate this book to my four veteran brothers. We were involved in a fight with our Mess Sargent while serving in Vietnam. That horrific experience changed our lives, and we haven't seen each other in 50+ years. No military action was taken to punish us for fighting. Instead, we were inhumanely treated like slaves and shipped off to five different units around Vietnam in the darkness of night. I will never stop fighting until I find them and get justice.

Pvt. Terry Brown

# **Table of Contents**

Chapter 1: How it All Started............................ 1

Chapter 2: US Army ........................................... 6

Chapter 3: Vietnam........................................... 10

Chapter 4: Dark Times..................................... 16

Chapter 5: Back in The States ......................... 30

Chapter 6: Hurricane Katrina.......................... 36

Chapter 7: 60-Year-Old Rapper..................... 40

## **Chapter 1: How it All Started**

This is a snapshot of my story and the injustices I experienced while serving the United States in the Vietnam War. Let me start by telling you how I ended up enlisting in the United States Army.

I was born and raised in New Orleans, Louisiana. My household consisted of my stepdad, mom, and two brothers, Ricardo and Jeffery Brown. In May 1968, my brother Rick and I were supposed to graduate from Joseph S. Clark High School, but I failed English. Consequently, I had to attend summer school.

We had a pool table at home. One day while shooting pool with my brothers and friends, we had to put one of our friends out because he lost his money and began acting irate.

A few days later, I got involved in a violent fight involving my friends after a graduation party on our block. This fight frightened our mom, so she sent Rick and I to live with our biological father, Ricardo Brown Sr., in Los Angeles, California.

We didn't know him too well since we hadn't seen or heard from him in years. Because of this move, I didn't finish high school or get my GED. Nonetheless, I was still optimistic because I was living in one of the greatest cities in the world.

Back in New Orleans, my brothers and I told people that our father was a painter, but he never touched a paintbrush. Our dad was a racehorse bookie. He always had a roll of money big enough to choke a camel.

It was crazy watching all these people lose their money to my dad. He always said, "I don't ask or tell them to bet. I'm just a way for them to bet without having to go to the track." At the time of the move, I was 17, and my brother was turning 19. We moved in with our dad, who remarried and had two kids with his new wife, Marion.

Regardless of his marital status, he also had a girlfriend named Marilyn. My father didn't try to hide his infidelity. He brought us to meet his mistress because he wanted to show off his kids.

That fucked me up and confused me so much that I kept mistakenly calling them each other's names. My dad was so pissed that he found us jobs at Lucky's supermarket, a car, and our own furnished apartment on Inglewood Blvd in the heart of LA. We were thrilled to be out on our own with nobody to tell us what to do. Life was truly amazing because we had no one to slow our roll.

I started hanging out in Watts and Compton with my cousin Lloyd Girard whose family moved from New Orleans when we were kids in the 1960s. I was introduced to cannabis after a high school football game in Pasadena, CA, with Lloyd. Lloyd had two brothers, Glen and Van, and two sisters, Denise and Cathy. They owned a few horses and would take me riding on them.

One time they entered me in a barrel racing contest at a rodeo, and I won $2^{nd}$ place. I loved spending time with my cousins whenever I wasn't working or at the track with Rick. He was in love with horse racing and was good at picking winners.

Los Angeles had two of the best racetracks in America, Santa Anita and Hollywood Park in downtown LA. Hollywood was where you would see all the big-time celebrities. We were taught to bet on horses by our stepdad, who had a book that talked all about it. That book was a gambler's bible. Using what he learned from that book, Rick started winning like crazy. He won so much that he quit his job at the supermarket.

Unfortunately, all good things must come to an end. Rick's luck got so bad that he had no other option but to join the US Air Force for four years of service. This left me in a bad spot because I couldn't move back to my mom's house in New Orleans or afford a place to live in LA. Therefore, I went with my brother to see the recruiter. When he said four years, that's too much time for me. I started speaking with an army recruiter. The recruiter told me that if I signed up for three years and took Stock Control and Accounting as my MOS (Military Occupational Specialist), I wouldn't see any part of Vietnam. MOS is what you would be trained to do while serving in the Army. Stock Control includes ordering supplies and shipping them to the troops. This sounded great to me and my dad, who was ready to get rid of me, so on December 6, 1968, at 18, I entered the U. S. Army for a three-year tour.

## **Chapter 2: US Army**

All my uncles served in the military, so it was a family thing, and we followed suit. Our Uncle Alverez retired from the Army and worked as an FBI Agent. Our uncle, who we always called Cowboy, retired from the Navy, and our Uncle Herman served in the Army. We didn't find out our Uncle Cowboy's real name until we were teenagers. Even today, I have friends I've known for decades, and I still don't know their real names. New Orleans is crazy like that. Our uncles inspired us to do well while serving in the military. I planned to make Sergeant by the time I finished serving.

I enlisted in Los Angeles, California, so they sent me to Fort Ore, California, for basic training. Basic was an eight-week training course designed to get you in physical shape to serve and learn how to take orders. One training routine was to sit on an empty beach and guard the sand with no one ever coming around. It trained you to never leave your post, no matter what.

Training was hell because the day started at 5:00 AM with a 5-mile run, more exercise, and then breakfast. After breakfast, we would train all day until we passed out. Even though training was hard, I gave it my all because I never liked finishing second. After graduating from basic training, I received my first promotion. I was so proud of myself because out of 80 men, only 3 received one.

Everyone had family and friends at the graduation except a few other men who couldn't hide their sadness and me. Most of my family was in New Orleans, and my dad had no intentions of coming. He was so glad that I was out of his way. His neglect didn't bother me because most of the stuff I learned about being a man was from my stepdad. I made many friends to party with after the ceremony, but it would have been nice to have some of my family there.

Next, it was time to head to Fort Lee, Virginia, for AIT (Advanced Individual Training). This was where I learned stock control and accounting. I was taught how to order, track, and ship supplies to the troops. I loved this because I wanted to become the hook-up man. I diligently learned everything I could about my new job.

This was a six-week course at Fort Lee, Virginia, in March. There was a snowstorm that caused over 4ft of snow. This amazed the men from the south, who started jumping out the windows to play in the snow. Of course, I was one of them. We had never seen snow, and to see so much at one time blew our minds.

After a few moments of pure joy, the cold ran us back inside. That's one memory I will never forget. I never saw snow like that again. I was trying to finish top in my class but ended up finishing third. That led to another promotion. I was finally done with all my training and officially a United States soldier, Specialist 3. I was given 30 days leave to await orders for my next duty station.

## **Chapter 3: Vietnam**

I returned to New Orleans in April of 1969, and it was time to cross paths with the guys I fought on my block. I could see the admiration for me in people's eyes while they checked out my uniform. I had become a man while most of my former peers were still playing in the streets. Everyone looked at me differently, including my family. I enjoyed my time with everyone back home, talking about LA life and my time in the military.

The day my orders came, my family gathered around to hear where I would be stationed. I was hoping for Germany, Japan, or Hawaii, where fewer casualties occurred. Everyone was so excited that I decided to let my mom read the letter to us.

As she started reading, her face dropped along with the letter. Then she started crying as if she had lost a family member. The letter read:

"You are to report to San Francisco, California, for deployment to Southeast Asia (Vietnam)."

There was no way this could be possible because of the promise the recruiter told me. Regardless of the broken promise, there was nothing I could do about it. I was 18 years old and headed to hell.

It was so hard leaving my mother and my family, not knowing if I would ever see them again. My little brother and I had a heated argument the day before my deployment. He was devastated about me going to the war. My pain cut even deeper because our last conversation before we went our separate ways in the war was an argument.

My stepdad never said much, but when he spoke, I listened closely because he was one of the wisest people I know. Before leaving, he pulled me aside and said, "I'm very proud of you. Although I'm not your real dad, you are my real son." I responded, "You taught me everything I know. You are ten times better than my real dad."

I made it to Frisco, and it was time to load the plane. No one had anything to say. The entire trip to Nam (Vietnam) was silent. It was so quiet that you could hear a rat pissing on cotton.

The flight took 18+ hours, so we stopped in Japan to refuel. I wasn't allowed to buy a beer because I was still underage. Nonetheless, I was still headed to war, with my life in danger.

We finally arrived in Vietnam, but the airport was under attack, so the plane had to keep flying until the assault was over. I experienced scary times and hadn't even landed yet. We were rushed off to our temporary living quarters once we landed.

I spent most of my first few days in Vietnam burning human waste. There was no sewerage system at the airport, so we had to take a long hook and drag all the tubs from the port-a-lets to a large field where we would fill them up with gasoline and set them on fire.

For three days, all I smelled was burning shit. This was hell on earth. Burning shit smells ten times worse than regular shit. I prayed every day that they would send me to my new station. Finally, after the three shittiest days of my life, I was sent to my new home, and I could not have been happier.

My new home was at $1^{st}$ Logistics Company, USARY, in Qunion, Vietnam. I oversaw the supply room, which was right up my alley. Everyone wanted to be my buddy so they could get their supplies faster. I was finally the hook-up man that I desired to be. Life was great. Almost everyone had a reel-to-reel music player, and music would be blasting every night. After work, all the brothers and Mexicans would meet at the basketball court for smoke sessions. The weed was potent in Nam. We all carried pipes because it rained too much to smoke papers. During a specific time of the year called monsoon season, it never stopped raining. Then the rain would shut off like a valve, and the sun would take over. That's why they have such a beautiful rainforest.

The company I worked for supplied troops that were fighting in the fields. On many occasions, we would ride downtown to party with the local Vietnamese that couldn't get onto our base. They needed special clearance to be allowed on base. We would load a 2.5-ton truck with GIs, go downtown Quinion, and party. Sometimes we would bring a carton of cigarettes to Papa San. That would get us a lady for the day, and you could smoke Opium with him all day. That was the best deal ever. We would have sex, smoke, and then have more sex.

After being in the country for a few months, I began talking to a lady dating a white captain who took great care of her. He purchased her a refrigerator and a TV, which was rare at the time. She was beautiful, but I was able to steal her heart. Whenever her man had to work, I would creep over and spend the night.

One night when she was bathing me outside in a barrow, kids started gathering by the fence, so I asked her what was up. She said they were waiting to see me grow a tail. White men had told them that black people grow tails at midnight. I threw a bar of soap at them and ran them off. So much crazy shit happened during wartime.

## **Chapter 4: Dark Times**

It was now July 1969, and we were returning to base after visiting downtown when we started receiving sniper fire. Hearing those bullets hitting that truck caused someone to stand up. I reached up to pull him back down, but the driver swiftly shifted gears and caused us to fly off the back of the truck.

I woke up in the hospital with head and shoulder injuries. I never saw the other guy again because he was sent to a major hospital in Saigon, which is now the capital of Vietnam. Because I tried to save his life, I was given a Bronze Star and another promotion to an E-4. I was well on my way to making Sergeant before my retirement date.

I had only been in the Army for seven months and still had 28 months left to serve. At this point, my career was going so well that I started setting my sights on making E-6 by the time I retired. Despite my injuries and the fact that I was living through hell, life was amazing.

Because of a sniper attack, we were ordered to refrain from going downtown, so we started having parties at the EM Club on base. They would bring bands and dancers to entertain us at the club. An EM club means Enlisted Men only. In other words, no officers are allowed.

One night after one of these parties, the Mess Sergeant decided to take the band, dancers, and some of his friends to the mess hall for late-night snacks. We thought we could join them, but when we got to the door, the Mess Sergeant stopped us and yelled, "No niggers allowed!" Then pushed us back and tried to lock the door.

We weren't having it, so a fight ensued. Then we took all the food to the basketball court and began having our own party. Before we got to eat the food, the MPs (Military

Police) arrived on jeeps with machine guns locked and loaded.

They arrested five of us. Instead of taking military action for fighting, they locked us up in manmade jails while they figured out what to do with us. They kept us locked up for three days without a word on our punishment. We were supposed to receive an Article 15 or a Court Martial. I would have only lost one stripe, which I could have quickly earned back. Instead, they shipped us five off in the dark of night with only the clothes on our backs in five different directions and units around Vietnam. That was a similar strategy slave owners used on rebellious slaves.

This was not supposed to happen to someone serving their country in a time of war. They also changed our MOS, which was what we were trained to do while in Vietnam. I never saw those four men again, and I still don't know what happened to them. They've been on my mind heavily over the past 50+ years.

Next, I was flown to 510 Engineers, a company located in Plaque, Vietnam. It was extremely cold, but I was sent there without a jacket or directions to find my new company. I asked around the airport and was told to go to Engenders Hill.

I caught a ride up there to find out they only have 501 to 509 companies on the hill. I returned to the airport and asked around some more, but no one knew of the 510 company, so I did the only thing I could think of. I returned to my old company, where I was arrested and charged with AWOL on arrival. They took military action, gave me my first Article 15 on August 14, 1969, and removed one of my stripes.

That severely affected my mental health and my feelings about the Army. I was sent back to look for 510 Company under armed guard in handcuffs. It was embarrassing, to say the least.

My escort asked around the airport and was told the same thing I was told. Go to the hill and check there. I was laughing inside so hard because I knew it wasn't there and I wasn't about to tell him. It wasn't like he would have believed me anyway.

I enjoyed the ride because I knew we would return to the airport shortly. Once back at the airport, he couldn't find any information on where the 510 Company was located, so he was ready to return to Quinon.

We were about to return when suddenly someone passed with a sign that read, "I'm here to pick up the new captain for the 510 company." Talk about bad luck. So now he just sat around waiting for my new company commander to arrive so he could sign me over to him.

First impressions mean the world. I unjustly met my new commander in handcuffs, and he immediately read me the Riot Act and sternly said, "I will not put up with any of your antics, and you will obey my orders," as if I had already caused him stress and misery. Then my handcuffs were removed, and we took a long ride to 510 in the valley.

This was a new company deep in the wilderness. That's why we couldn't find it. My new company was 88% white, but the transportation company across the field was 85% black. This is where I ended up spending all my time when I wasn't working.

My new job was to perform guard duty at the ammo dump. Most of the men in 510 Company were engineers. Guard duty was alright, except for the nights we would get attacked. When things were going good with no attacks, we would ride and race the forklifts. The forklifts were enormous because they had to move large containers of ammo. The tires were the size of an SUV, so you had to climb a ladder to get in one.

For guard duty, we would take little vials of speed to make sure we wouldn't fall asleep at work. One night, while on duty, we began receiving enemy fire, and a sniper shot someone on a forklift. The victim was between my tower and another guy's tower. We both climbed down to get him off the forklift before he got shot again.

Once he was on the ground, we tried to stop his bleeding, but it wasn't working. We screamed for a medic. Once they arrived, we had to get back in our towers. I never found out what happened to him, but I don't think he survived.

The visualization of seeing someone get shot down kept replaying in my head like a reoccurring nightmare. After that night, I couldn't sleep. I kept seeing the slain soldier in a puddle of blood every time I closed my eyes.

I was ordered to go back and work guard duty at the ammo dump. I informed my commander that I wasn't getting any sleep because of those nightmares and could fall asleep while on guard duty and risk everyone's life.

I was told to suck it up, soldier, and go do my job. To keep from losing my mind, I went AWOL for real this time. I went to stay with the brothers across the field in the transportation company for a few days while I figured things out. I just knew I couldn't go back to that ammo dump.

I returned to my 510 company and told my commander there was no way I would return to that ammo dump, so we had to figure something out. After lengthy discussions, I talked him into transferring me to the transportation company to ride shotgun on convoys.

My new job involved carrying an M-79 grenade launcher and an M-16 machine gun while riding conveys. This allowed me to see a lot of the country and many villages. Things were great, even though we would sometimes receive sniper fire.

I'll never forget the day we rode into one town, and the Koreans had cut a Vietcong down the middle and hung him in the middle of town to make an example of him. These were the nightmares of war. The Koreans didn't play. They were not under the Geneva Convention, which was established for international legal standards for humanitarian treatment during the war. Not being a part of that convention allowed them to do unlawful things to their prisoners. Cutting a man in half and hanging him out for all to see is out of control, even during a war. Today I can still see that image.

After that experience, I was further tormented mentally and ready for a new job again. In January 1970, I received orders to report to Saigon and my new duty station. Thankfully, I only had a few months left to serve in Vietnam. At this point, I was considered a short-timer and given a short walking cane. My mind was in terrible shape, and my heart was in the dumps. This was when I was introduced to heroin.

Saigon was like being back in the USA. Ladies were driving around in convertibles, and some even had afros. I thought I had died and gone to heaven. There was an area called Truman and Key, which didn't allow any white people. This was where I took my first ride on that white horse (heroin).

When I saw the state of mind these vets were in, I had to get there. They were going through the most but seemed happy. I started by skin poppin. That is when they just put the needle under your skin and not in your veins. It didn't do anything for me, so I went for the main line.

All of my problems rushed to the front of my mind. While I anticipated for my problems to be relieved and the heroin to be disbursed through veins, I yelled, "Put it in my blood, so I can feel like the rest of these men!"

When I tell you that my first ride was a motherfucker. I found out why people stay addicted. It's a feeling unlike any other. Your body goes into a state of unconsciousness, and you enter a world of numbness. I was now an addict, but I wasn't seeing bodies and blood every night.

I was fighting to save my sanity. If using drugs was the only way I could do this, then shoot me up! I was there from January till April and used heroin often. This was the purest heroin with very little cut on it.

When April arrived, it was time for me to return to the United States. I was headed home with a monkey on my back (addicted to heroin). It was dehumanizing to return home in that condition.

I was given 30 days leave while awaiting orders for my next station. I didn't want my mother to see me like this, but I had no choice. As soon as my mother saw me, she broke down crying because she instantly saw the damage the war had done to me. Many parents across the country endured that same experience of seeing their children return home from the war damaged in several ways.

Her exact words to me were, "what have they done to my baby?!" I was loaded out of my mind while she cried to the skies. Because the drugs were cut so much in America, I had to shoot up a lot more to satisfy my needs. This wasn't good because I still had twenty months left to serve in the Army.

It was time to find out where I would be heading to finish serving my tour. I was ordered to report to Fort Carson, Colorado, Btry B 1st Bn 19th Arty 5th Inf United States Army, where they trained troops to go to war. I wondered why the hell they would send me there when I had plans to return to Vietnam. It was as if they were trying to drive me crazy. Previously, I didn't get proper training before being sent to war.

The drugs helped me with the nightmares, but they were all coming back because of the training exercises. We would go out on bivouac (overnight in the woods) and play war games where we would shoot at each other with BB guns. This was bringing back all the nightmares of the war, and I couldn't take it. I tried talking to my company commander, but he said the same thing I was told in Nam. "You are a soldier in the United States Army, and you will follow orders! End of story."

Once again, my sanity was tested, and I went AWOL again. From June 8 - June 12, 1970, I was AWOL in Colorado, hiding out by some friends. When I returned, I was given my 3$^{rd}$ Article 15 and demoted to an E-1. After talking with the company commander, I was sent to see the doctor, who offered me an undesirable discharge under conditions other than honorable. I was filled with rage and hate because my compensation for all the shit I experienced was paperwork that economically castrated me and unjustly affected my reputation.

When your mind is at stake, you do what's necessary to survive. My discharge papers stated, "There is no psychiatric condition which would warrant separation under current medical provisions at this time. You have a passive-aggressive personality disorder."

## Chapter 5: Back in The States

Ten years later, PTSD was created for veterans of the Afghanistan War. With all this being said, I accepted their offer and took the bad discharge. They sent me back to New Orleans and told me never to step foot on any military base again. That didn't bother me because I was done dealing with the U. S. Army and just wanted to move on with my life.

I was now a disgraced veteran with a bad discharge and heading back home addicted to drugs. Once back home, I couldn't live at my mom's house using heroin, so I started living on the streets in empty apartments.

Parkchester Apartment complex was under repair, so it became my new community. After a year of this lifestyle, I finally cleaned up my act, got off heroin, and started hustling hard to make ends meet and turn things around.

I was a taxicab driver, a delivery man for Light Bulb Delivery, a delivery man for Coke, a haul carrier for brick layers, a machinist for the space shuttle at the Michoud facility, and a phone repairman with Western Electric. Every year I started a new job, constantly looking for the job of my dreams.

I fought relentlessly for ten years before getting my discharge upgraded to under honorable conditions. That allowed me to apply for federal jobs and employment with the US Post Office in 1980. This was my dream job, but there was a problem.

I had calcium spurs growing on both of my heels. I figured that while I had a sit-down job at Western Electric repairing phones, I would have them removed. I never dreamed I would get a call from the post office before my heels healed.

While I was healing, the post office called me in for an interview. When the interviewer saw me come in on crutches, he said, "I have good news and bad news. The good news is that you have the job. The bad news is that you have to start in three weeks."

I went straight home and cut off my cast. I was so desperate for this job and wasn't going to let the opportunity pass me by. I just had my daughter and would do whatever it took to make sure she had a good life. When I started delivering mail, my first route was in the St. Thomas Project.

All new employees had to start on the worst routes. Because my feet didn't have time to heal from the operation, I had a terrible limp. The kids in the projects used to yell to their mothers, "Here comes the disabled mailman!"

Those kids were heartless, but it wasn't like they were lying. I walked like I was crippled, but nothing was going to stop me from being a mailman. After three years, I was able to get my own route, but I would be working for a terrible supervisor who was thirsty to make a name for himself.

I took the route because I was tired of working bad and dangerous routes. I figured as long as I did my job, it wouldn't be a problem. In less than three months on my new route, my supervisor started harassing me daily.

That intensified my PTSD. To keep from killing him, I called my aunt and told her to tell my mom to come to my house. Then I called the Times Picayune Newspaper and the New Orleans Police Department to tell them there was a man on a roof on Piety Drive with a gun.

Then I climbed on my roof with a gun, a pillow for my hemorrhoids, and a bag for hyperventilation. I smoked a joint while I waited for the police to arrive. When the first police car arrived, I ate the last piece of my joint.

Not long after the police arrived, my mother, Father Rogers, and the postmaster arrived. I stayed on that roof for 5+ hours, talking to the police about what I was doing on the roof. I informed them about my fight with PTSD and my supervisor. The postmaster promised me I would keep my job and won't continue working for that supervisor again.

Then my mother climbed the ladder and said, "Look, MF! I didn't raise a quitter. Now throw that damn gun down, and let's work this shit out!" My mom was as real as it gets and didn't play. Her nickname was Battling Bern.

After that, I threw the gun to the ground. While coming down, I thought I was going to jail or a mental institution, but nope. First, the police left with the gun. Next, Father Rogers left, and then it was just my mother and me.

I spent the night at my mother's house after soaking in hot water to help heal my hemorrhoids. I was ordered to see a psychiatrist before returning to work. After two visits, the doctor told me I didn't have to return to work until I was ready. I received full pay, so I stayed out for three months.

When I returned to work, I was allowed to select my new supervisor. I chose to work at Chef Station for Woodrow Still and Raymond Guillot. After working with them for a few years, I was offered a detail at the main office. I worked my way up to supervisor. Before I retired, I became an assistant to the Postmaster of New Orleans. I fought for ten years to get my discharge upgraded to honorable conditions and four years to get my PTSD approved. In 2004, I won my case for PTSD, and I was able to retire from the post office with my disability.

## Chapter 6: Hurricane Katrina

In 2005, I lost everything in Hurricane Katrina and had to move to Houston, Texas. My mother and stepdad were living with me. I couldn't afford to take care of them, so I moved them to Los Angeles, California, to be close to my brothers Rick and Jeff.

While living in Houston, my depression got worse every day. My family was spread all over America, but I was the only one in Houston. God works in mysterious ways, and through people we come across throughout our journeys. I was going through the unthinkable again during and after Hurricane Katrina. Then a blessing came out of nowhere.

The CEO of Barnes & Noble Bookstore, Louis Riggio, Tony Bennett, and several others created the Home Again Foundation and blessed 100 families with homes to move back to New Orleans. I was blessed to receive one on St. Bernard Ave in the 7$^{th}$ ward of New

Orleans and meet the Riggio family and Mr. Tony Bennett.

Rooms-To-Go furnished all these houses. All we had to do was sign over our old lots that were destroyed in Hurricane Katrina. It saved my life because I was going crazy living in Houston post-Katrina.

I was finally back in my city, living with my daughter and several family members. I had a 25 ft. party barge that we used to go fishing on. When the Saints won the Superbowl, we turned the boat into a float and rode in the parade. It was an amazing time, but changes were on the horizon.

Months later, a terrible oil spill killed many fish and affected the surrounding environment. After that, I decided to move to LA, where my mother and brothers lived.

I moved to Duarte, California, and things started off great. I moved into a senior citizen apartment to save on rent. After living there for a few months, things started changing.

The lady in charge didn't like that some of the tenants started a prayer group in the clubhouse. The manager started harassing and closing the clubhouse early. For Christmas, she closed it for two weeks. She put some bad energy in the air during the Christmas season and negatively affected everyone's mood. I wrote on all the walls of my apartment. Then I called the VA to tell them I was having some challenges with my mental health. It felt like some of the people employed to help us did the opposite.

After calling the VA, I left the apartment and lived on the streets of Los Angeles for three days. I needed a break from the environment I lived in. When I returned, the manager started screaming, "he's going to kill me! Call the police! Hurry! Hurry!" I started laughing and told the staff to tell the police I would be sitting at the bus stop.

Before I knew it, three police cars came flying up the street. They took me into the apartment and explained that I would have to pay for all the damages and that I couldn't stay in my apartment anymore because of what I wrote on the bathroom walls. I wrote, "sometimes I feel like burning this MF down." Because of that, I had to return to New Orleans and regroup.

## **Chapter 7: 60-Year-Old Rapper**

My life dramatically shifted for the better in 2011 when I created a song called Bad Knee. It went viral and put me in the position to connect with many people and have a creative outlet. I prayed that my popularity would help me find my friends I lost that night in Vietnam.

I went around New Orleans doing my song and dance to see how people liked it. They loved it so much that I decided to go to Atlanta to promote it. I would stand on the back of a convertible mustang and perform Bad Knee.

One time the Atlanta police pulled up on me in front of Gladys Knight's Restaurant while I was standing on the back of a mustang. They told me to get down or go to jail. Of course, I got my old ass down. Before they left, one of the officers said, "you must be from New Orleans."

After that trip, I had to see if I could make another song the people would like. I waited six months for my nephew and producer Kellen (prov-on-da-track) Smith to give me a beat. My first song made it to Worldstar and propelled me to new heights, so I cared a lot about my follow-up song. He wanted me to collaborate with two of his rappers, but I wrote my next track for myself. The beat he gave me was perfect, and we made magic happen again. At this point, I realized I could really do this. So, I packed up and moved to California to promote my music and continue the pursuit of finding my four friends from Vietnam.

I moved back and forth from New Orleans to Los Angeles. At one point, I traveled to Atlanta, hoping to get my story told. I became friends with Nick Valencia, a reporter for CNN. He took me to their headquarters for a tour and to meet some of his co-workers. This was amazing because I just knew we were about to break my story on CNN. Wow, God's power was about to be seen by the world.

Suddenly, Donald Trump began dominating their headlines, and nothing else could hit their airways. It wasn't time. This showed that I had more work to do. All things happen in God's timing.

In 2015, I was blessed with the opportunity to be featured on Snoop Dogg's Thanksgiving Day Special. What an honor. In 2018, I was living in Denver, Colorado, but the weather ran me off. I moved back to Los Angeles to be close to my mother. The day after I moved back to California, my mother died. I never even got to see her.

In 2019, I moved back to Louisiana right before the pandemic started. I am still working to keep growing the name Unc Imo. In the meantime, I had it on my heart to write and release this book. Please review my work under Uncimo on all social sites. My YouTube is full of my journey getting to this point. Be sure to check out the video of when I was kicked out of Uber for smoking pot. Also, check out my songs which include Bad Knee, Deep in da Game, Best Friend, Juke Joint, They Get High, IDGAF, Do dat Dance, The Prayer, Step it up, Bust it up, and Back 2 Back. I will find my brothers, or I'll die trying. Please have Respect for All Veterans.

In conclusion, I was blessed with my daughter Trea. God sent her to save my life. I was living a drug-infested life because of my earlier addiction to heroin. No more heroin, but I was using everything else, including acid, angel dust, pills, cough syrup, and whatever else I could get my hands on. My plight is similar to many veterans who didn't get the opportunity to tell their stories. I hope to provide a sense of understanding for our trials and tribulations and be a voice for the voiceless. I thank God every day for my daughter and my life.

Made in the USA
Middletown, DE
07 March 2023